THE 10

Most Defining Moments of the Civil War Era

Myra Junyk

Series Editor
Jeffrey D. Wilhelm

Much thought, debate, and research went into choosing and ranking the 10 items in each book in this series. We realize that everyone has his or her own opinion of what is most significant, revolutionary, amazing, deadly, and so on. As you read, you may agree with our choices, or you may be surprised — and that's the way it should be!

Franklin Watts

an imprint of

 SCHOLASTIC

www.scholastic.com/librarypublishing

A Rubicon book published in association with Scholastic Inc.

Rubicon © 2008 Rubicon Publishing Inc.
www.rubiconpublishing.com

10 is a trademark of The 10 Books

Associate Publishers: Kim Koh, Miriam Bardswich
Project Editor: Amy Land
Editorial Assistant: Jessica Rose
Creative Director: Jennifer Drew
Project Manager/Designer: Jeanette MacLean
Graphic Designer: Doug Baines

The publisher gratefully acknowledges the following for permission to reprint copyrighted material in this book.

Every reasonable effort has been made to trace the owners of copyrighted material and to make due acknowledgment. Any errors or omissions drawn to our attention will be gladly rectified in future editions.

Cover image: *First at Vicksburg*–Courtesy U.S. Army Center of Military History

Library and Archives Canada Cataloguing in Publication

Junyk, Myra
    The 10 most defining moments of the Civil War era / Myra Junyk.

Includes index.
ISBN 978-1-55448-518-5

    1. Readers (Elementary). 2. Readers--United States--History--Civil War, 1861-1865. I. Title. II. Title: Ten most defining moments of the Civil War.

PE1117.J9612 2007   428.6   C2007-906686-0

1 2 3 4 5 6 7 8 9 10   10   17 16 15 14 13 12 11 10 09 08

Printed in Singapore

Contents

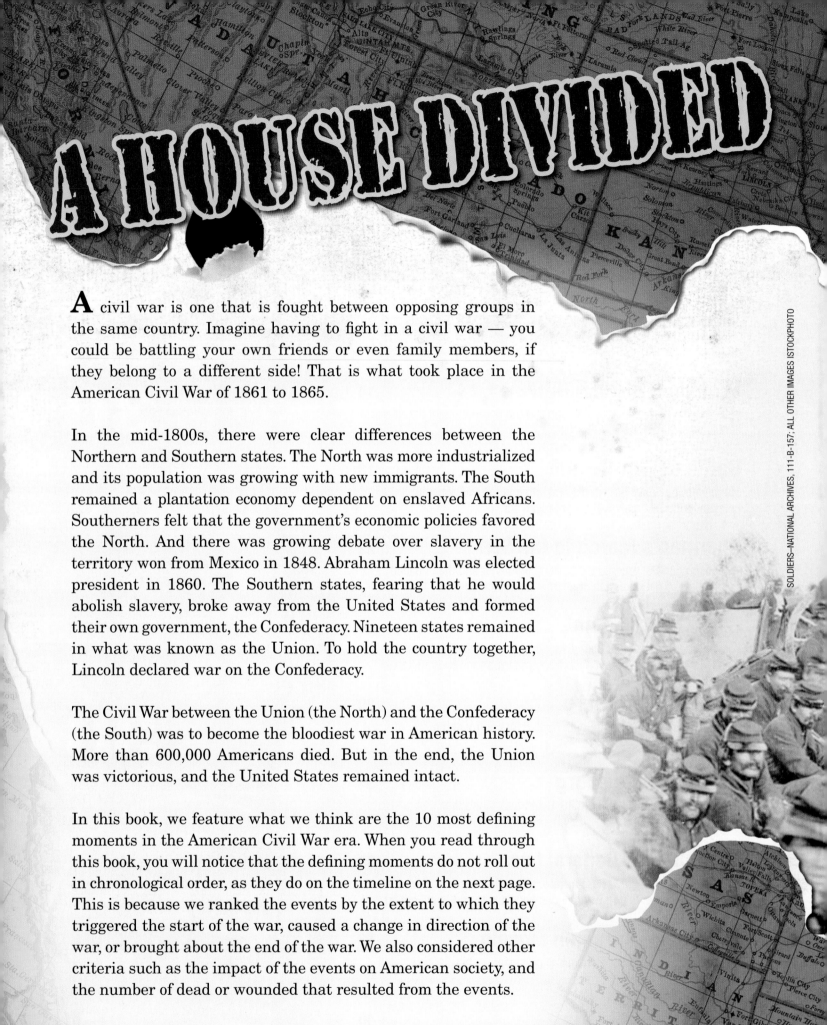

A HOUSE DIVIDED

A civil war is one that is fought between opposing groups in the same country. Imagine having to fight in a civil war — you could be battling your own friends or even family members, if they belong to a different side! That is what took place in the American Civil War of 1861 to 1865.

In the mid-1800s, there were clear differences between the Northern and Southern states. The North was more industrialized and its population was growing with new immigrants. The South remained a plantation economy dependent on enslaved Africans. Southerners felt that the government's economic policies favored the North. And there was growing debate over slavery in the territory won from Mexico in 1848. Abraham Lincoln was elected president in 1860. The Southern states, fearing that he would abolish slavery, broke away from the United States and formed their own government, the Confederacy. Nineteen states remained in what was known as the Union. To hold the country together, Lincoln declared war on the Confederacy.

The Civil War between the Union (the North) and the Confederacy (the South) was to become the bloodiest war in American history. More than 600,000 Americans died. But in the end, the Union was victorious, and the United States remained intact.

In this book, we feature what we think are the 10 most defining moments in the American Civil War era. When you read through this book, you will notice that the defining moments do not roll out in chronological order, as they do on the timeline on the next page. This is because we ranked the events by the extent to which they triggered the start of the war, caused a change in direction of the war, or brought about the end of the war. We also considered other criteria such as the impact of the events on American society, and the number of dead or wounded that resulted from the events.

Civil War Timeline

1850	Compromise of 1850
1859	Execution of John Brown
1860	Election of Abraham Lincoln
1861	Battle of Fort Sumter
1862	Battle of Antietam
1863	• Battle of Gettysburg • Battle of Vicksburg
1864	Sherman's March to the Sea
1865	• Surrender of General Lee • Assassination of Abraham Lincoln

WHAT WAS THE MOST DEFINING MOMENT OF THE CIVIL WAR ERA?

President Lincoln was shot only five days after the surrender of the Confederacy.

LINCOLN-LOC_LC-USZ62-8813; THEATER-LOC_LC-DIG-CWPB-02962

ABRAHAM LINCOLN

HEADLINE: President Shot! Dies from Head Wound — April 14, 1865

IMPACT: Loss of Lincoln's leadership for rebuilding the nation

The Civil War had finally ended with the surrender by the Confederates from the South. A brutal war had ripped the nation apart. President Lincoln was looking forward to the Reconstruction, a period of reunification of the two sides. But it was not to be. On the evening of April 14, 1865, only five days after the surrender of the South, President Lincoln and his wife were watching a play at Ford's Theatre in Washington. Just after 10:00 PM, John Wilkes Booth, a well-known actor, entered the theater. But he was not there to act. He was there to murder. Booth was a strong supporter of the Confederacy and he hated everything that President Lincoln stood for.

Lincoln and his wife were seated in the presidential box. When the president's bodyguard left his seat, Booth saw his chance. At 10:15 PM, Booth stepped into the box. He took aim and shot the president in the head. Lincoln slumped forward. Booth jumped onto the stage from the balcony. He broke his leg as he landed, but he was still able to escape from the theater.

Six soldiers carried Lincoln to a house across the street. Doctors worked to save him but could not remove the bullet from his brain. Nine hours later, the president was dead.

ASSASSINATION OF ABRAHAM LINCOLN

MAKING NEWS!

Booth shot the president at close range. Five doctors worked on the president throughout the night, but he never regained consciousness. Abraham Lincoln died at 7:22 AM on April 15, 1865, at the age of 56. His wife and son were among those at his bedside. "Now he belongs to the ages," declared Secretary of War Edwin M. Stanton. Booth was hunted down and shot by U.S. cavalry when he was found hiding in a barn near Bowling Green, Virginia, on April 26.

? How do you think Lincoln could have been protected? How has security changed for U.S. presidents over the years?

Quick Fact

The Treasury set up the Secret Service in 1865 not to protect the president, but to investigate counterfeiting. It wasn't until 1901 that the Secret Service was put in charge of protecting the president. This was after the assassination of two more presidents — Garfield in 1881 and McKinley in 1901.

This is the chair Lincoln was seated in when he was assassinated by John Wilkes Booth.

DEFINING MOMENT

The country faced great challenges after the war. How would the South be brought back into the Union? How would four million formerly enslaved Africans be treated? Lincoln had promised "malice towards none, charity for all." Now he was dead. Andrew Johnson was sworn in as president.

IN THE END ...

Lincoln's assassination right after the end of the Civil War was to have a big impact on the Reconstruction. This was the period in which Confederate states were brought back into the Union. Lincoln's successor, President Andrew Johnson from Tennessee was a former owner of enslaved Africans. He fought against many of the reforms for civil rights introduced by Congress. And Southern states introduced Black Codes. These were laws that limited the freedom of formerly enslaved Africans and counteracted new laws introduced by Congress granting rights to African Americans. A century later, African Americans were still fighting for civil rights laws for protection.

malice: *hatred; cruelty*

The Expert Says...

"Lincoln's achievements — saving the Union and freeing the [enslaved Africans] — and his martyrdom just at the war's end ensured his lasting fame.

— Mark E. Neely Jr., Professor of Civil War History, Pennsylvania State University

martyrdom: *dying violently for a cause*

10   **9**   **8**   **7**   **6**

Lincoln's ASSASSIN

Read this profile to discover more about the man who committed this shocking crime.

NAME:
John Wilkes Booth

BIRTH:
May 10, 1838

CAREER:
Acting — toured all over America and fell even more in love with the South

WARTIME ACTIVITY:
Smuggling medical supplies from the North to Confederate troops

ASSASSINATION PLOT:
Booth decided to shoot Lincoln after a kidnapping attempt failed. His accomplices were to kill Secretary of State William Seward and Vice President Johnson — the next two in line for president. Seward was stabbed but survived. No one followed through with Johnson. Booth wanted to kill the Union General Ulysses S. Grant as well, but Grant couldn't make it to the play.

CAUSE OF BOOTH'S DEATH:
Gunshot wound to the neck

? Much of the Civil War was fought in the South. What problems do you think the South faced after the war?

Take Note

The assassination of President Lincoln was a defining moment in the aftermath of the war. It ranks #10. The nation had lost a great leader at a time when he was most needed — to bring the two opposing sides back together as one nation and to ensure that formerly enslaved Africans were given the same rights as other Americans.
- Lincoln once said that he would "rather be assassinated" than surrender the ideals of the Declaration of Independence. What do you think might have been different if Lincoln had not been killed?

This engraving shows Kentucky Senator Henry Clay addressing the Senate. Senator Daniel Webster from Massachusetts is seated to the left of Clay, and John C. Calhoun is to the left of the Speaker's chair.

OF 1850

HEADLINE: Slavery Outlawed in Some States — Not Others! Fugitive Slave Act Is Part of the Compromise — September 18, 1850

IMPACT: Enslaved Africans who ran away could be brought back from Northern states and returned to slavery. The Compromise angered abolitionists and tension mounted in the nation.

Before the Civil War began, there were many years of debate over slavery. This debate grew as the United States gained new territory. In 1848, at the end of the Mexican-American War, the U.S. won the area that includes present-day California, Nevada, Utah, most of Arizona, and parts of New Mexico, Colorado, and Wyoming.

In 1849, the California Gold Rush brought many people to the area. California would soon become a state. Would it be a slave state or a free state? What would happen with the rest of the western territory won from Mexico in 1848?

Which states would become more powerful — the antislavery Northern states or the proslavery Southern states? For 10 weeks in 1850, Congress debated the issue. The result was a compromise. Several laws guaranteed a balance between slave states and free states.

The part of the Compromise of 1850 that raised the most protest was the Fugitive Slave Act. This law was passed to punish anyone caught helping runaway enslaved Africans. Abolitionists were furious. They promised to help these people in any way they could. The Compromise spurred abolitionists into action, a defining moment that would lead to war a decade later.

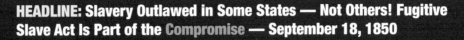

compromise: settlement between two extreme positions
abolitionists: people who work to end slavery

COMPROMISE OF 1850

MAKING NEWS!

A compromise is an attempt to please both sides of opposing groups. Congress tried to do this with the Compromise of 1850. To please the North, the Compromise stated that California would join the Union as a free state. Also, the slave trade would be abolished in Washington, D.C. To please the South, there would be no laws against slavery in the western territories of New Mexico and Utah. There would also be a tougher law when it came to capturing people who tried to escape from slavery.

DEFINING MOMENT

Many Americans believed that the Compromise of 1850 was a victory for national unity. But Northern abolitionists hated the Fugitive Slave Act. When it passed, there were about 20,000 people in the North who had escaped from slavery. All of them could now be recaptured! The Compromise was a defining moment in the buildup to war. The antislavery forces in the North began to increase their efforts to end slavery. The South threatened to break away if the Compromise did not go through. This tension would grow and send the country into a civil war.

IN THE END ...

Abolitionists extended the Underground Railroad to help enslaved Africans escape to Canada, which did not have slavery. People hid runaways at secret stations — their own homes and other safe places — and helped them travel to the next station. Many people protested the law. Harriet Beecher Stowe wrote her antislavery novel *Uncle Tom's Cabin* in 1852. Abraham Lincoln spoke out against slavery for many years before his election in 1860. The time for compromise ended with his election!

? Find out more about the plot of *Uncle Tom's Cabin*. How do you think people in the South felt about the book? How do people feel about it today?

Harriet Beecher Stowe

The Expert Says...

" The Southern states expressly approved the compromise in specially elected state conventions, but they warned grimly that a breakdown of the agreement would result in secession. "

— Charles P. Roland, Civil War historian

secession: withdrawal

Quick Fact

When Lincoln met Harriet Beecher Stowe, the author of *Uncle Tom's Cabin*, he is reported to have said, "So you're the little woman who wrote the book that started this great war."

FIGHTING WORDS!

The Compromise of 1850 led to very strong feelings on both sides of the slavery debate. Here are some of the most memorable quotations about the event.

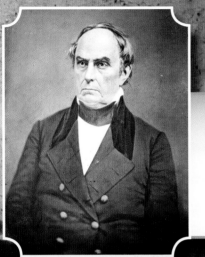

"I wish to speak today, not as a Massachusetts man, not as a Northern man, but as an American. … I speak today for the preservation of the Union."

— Senator Daniel Webster from Massachusetts

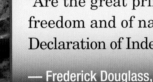

"Are the great principles of political freedom and of natural justice … in the Declaration of Independence extended to us?"

— Frederick Douglass, abolitionist

"Let the President drench our land of freedom in blood, but he will never make us obey that law."

— Congressman Joshua Giddings from Ohio

Quick Fact

Senator Henry Clay from Kentucky was 72 years old when he helped put together the Compromise of 1850. He had been an owner of enslaved Africans since the age of five, but hated slavery and wanted it abolished.

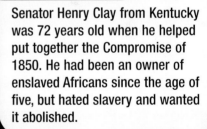

"How can the Union be saved? …[T]here is but one way by which it can be, and that is by adopting such measures as will satisfy the states belonging to the Southern section that they can remain in the Union consistently with their honor and safety."

— Senator John C. Calhoun from South Carolina

Take Note

The Compromise of 1850 takes the #9 spot. It opened up debate about slavery — an issue that stirred up anger and threats from both North and South. This unhappiness built until it eventually boiled over into war.
• Do some research. Find out the role that enslaved Africans played in the economy of the South. Why do you think the people in the North were antislavery while those in the South were proslavery?

5   4   3   2   1

John Brown was the first white American to stage a revolt against slavery.

JOHN BROWN

IMPACT: The hanging of Brown widened the split between the North and South.

John Brown was a leader of the antislavery movement in Kansas Territory. In May 1855, a proslavery group attacked the town of Lawrence, in Kansas. To get even, Brown and his group attacked and killed five settlers in the area. Violence continued in Kansas, but Brown moved to Virginia the next year.

Brown planned to start a slave revolt in Virginia. He formed a band of about 20 men, including five African Americans. In August 1859, he decided to raid the armory at Harpers Ferry for weapons. Many people tried to persuade him not to do it. Frederick Douglass, the famous African-American abolitionist, warned him, "You're walking into a perfect steel-trap and you will never get out alive."

On October 16 at 4:00 AM, Brown and his followers began their attack on Harpers Ferry by cutting the telegraph wires. They captured the armory and took 60 citizens hostage. They hoped the Africans enslaved by these hostages would join their revolt, but none did.

The local militia soon pinned down Brown's rebels and federal troops were called in. The uprising lasted only 36 hours. It was to cost John Brown his life and propel the nation toward a civil war.

---

treason: attempt to overthrow the government

EXECUTION OF JOHN BROWN

MAKING NEWS!

Under the command of Colonel Robert E. Lee, who later became a Confederate general, federal troops killed half of Brown's men and captured the rest. Brown was quickly tried in court for his attack on the armory. He faced charges of "murder, criminal conspiracy, and treason against the Commonwealth of Virginia." He and six of his followers were sentenced to hang.

conspiracy: *plot involving two or more people*

? Do you think Brown should have been executed for his actions? Why or why not?

In this painting, The Last Moments of John Brown by Thomas Hovenden, Brown stops to kiss a baby on his way to his execution.

DEFINING MOMENT

The execution of John Brown took place more than a year before the Civil War began. However, it played a defining role in splitting the nation apart. John Brown and his execution divided the nation into two sides — proslavery and antislavery. In the North, Brown became a hero "murdered" for his belief that slavery was evil and that it should end. In the South, fears were growing that antislavery protesters were prepared to use violence to destroy the Southern way of life.

IN THE END ...

The raid on Harpers Ferry was a dismal failure as an antislavery rebellion, but John Brown did achieve his goal. His trial and execution inspired Northern abolitionists to step up the fight against slavery. However, states in the South, fearful of more revolts and violence, began to reorganize the militia system. The Confederate Army was formed in 1861.

Quick Fact

John Brown rented the farmhouse where he prepared for the raid. He paid $35 in gold to the estate of Dr. Robert F. Kennedy. This was not the Robert F. Kennedy, brother of President John F. Kennedy, who worked for civil rights in the early 1960s.

The Expert Says...

This was the worst nightmare for some slaveholders, who were really increasingly convinced that the abolitionists were going to mount an invasion of the South.

— James Horton, Professor of American Studies and History, George Washington University

A PLEA FOR FREEDOM

Dangerfield Newby was the first of Brown's men to die in the raid at Harpers Ferry. Newby was born an enslaved African in 1815. Newby was later freed by his white father, but his wife and seven children were not. Newby was told he could buy the freedom of his wife and baby for $1,500 — a great deal of money in 1859. Newby joined John Brown, hoping to free his entire family. This letter from Newby's wife was found on his body.

Dear Husband,
I want you to buy me as soon as possible, for if you do not get me somebody else will.

. . . [T]he last two years have been like a troubled dream to me. It is said Master is in [need] of money. If so, I know not what time he may sell me, and then all my bright hopes of the future are blasted, for there has been one bright hope to cheer me in all my troubles, that is to be with you, for if I thought I should never see you, this earth would have no charms for me. Do all you can for me, which I have no doubt you will. I want to see you so much.

? Do you agree with Dangerfield Newby's decision to join Brown? Explain.

Take Note

Although John Brown's execution took place before the Civil War began, it was a defining moment on the road to war. This event takes the #8 spot. The tension between North and South that had started with the Compromise of 1850 reached a boiling point with increased fears of violence. The war was not far off.
• If you were Brown's lawyer, what arguments would you use to defend him in court?

Three 100-pounder Parrot Rifles, seen here, were used against Fort Sumter by the Union army to win back the fort.

MORRIS ISLAND CANNONS–LOC, LC-DIG-CWPB-04734

RT SUMTER

HEADLINE: It's War! Confederates Fire First Shots! April 12, 1861

IMPACT: President Lincoln called for an army of 500,000 to save the Union in a civil war.

In November 1860, Abraham Lincoln was elected the 16th president of the United States. The Southern states, fearing he would abolish slavery, decided to break away from the Union and start their own country, known as the Confederacy. On December 20, 1860, South Carolina became the first state to secede, or break away, from the United States. By the time Lincoln was sworn in as president in March 1861, six more states had left the Union. As these states broke away, they took over most of the federal forts in their states. Fort Sumter, an important fort in the harbor of Charleston, South Carolina, was an exception. It was still under Union control. But it was running out of supplies.

President Lincoln knew that if he sent supplies, the Confederates would attack the fort. But if he didn't, the Union soldiers in the fort would starve or be forced to surrender. Ultimately, Lincoln decided to send supplies.

The Confederates decided to attack before the supplies arrived. On April 12, 1861, at 4:30 AM, they opened fire on Fort Sumter. Major Robert Anderson had fewer than 100 men to protect the fort. They were no match for 50 cannons. Two days later, Fort Sumter was flying the Confederate flag!

 Do you agree with Lincoln's decision to send supplies? Explain.

BATTLE OF FORT SUMTER

MAKING NEWS!

The Confederates fired the first shot at Fort Sumter. It signaled the start of the Civil War. Confederate soldiers shelled the fort for more than 30 hours. Citizens of Charleston gathered on their rooftops to watch. More than 3,000 shells were shot, but no one was killed during the attack. With only 100 men in the fort, Major Anderson knew he could not hold out against this strong attack. On April 14, 1861, he called for a truce. The Union flag was taken down and the Confederacy flag was soon flying over the fort.

DEFINING MOMENT

The attack on Fort Sumter marked the beginning of the armed conflict between the North and the South. On April 15, 1861, Lincoln called for 75,000 soldiers to stop the rebellion of the Southern states. Two days later, Virginia joined the Confederacy. Within five weeks, three more states followed. As each state left the Union, volunteers signed up to fight for the new Confederacy. By July 4, Lincoln was calling for an army of 500,000 in the North to deal with the situation.

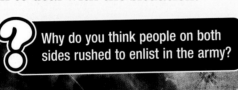
? Why do you think people on both sides rushed to enlist in the army?

IN THE END ...

The Battle of Fort Sumter was the first of many battles in a war that was to tear the nation apart, with families and friends fighting against one another. The rural foot soldiers of the South were believed to be better soldiers than many of the North's soldiers who came from urban areas. And the South hoped to gain support from Britain and France. However, the North had many advantages — it had a population of 22 million versus the South's 9 million, of whom 3.5 million were enslaved Africans. The North had more resources, with more than 80 percent of the nation's factories, more than half of its railways, and most of the shipyards. This industrial base would be a major reason for the North's victory.

Quick Fact

At the end of the war, Major Anderson returned to the fort to raise the very same flag, this time marking the Union victory over the Confederacy.

The only casualty of the first battle of the Civil War at Fort Sumter was a horse!

Bombardment of Fort Sumter, Charleston Harbor

The Expert Says...

" As time ran out for Anderson, it was also running out for Lincoln. His path was clear now. Both Sumter and Pickens [a fort in Florida] would be reinforced, and both re-supplied, he announced. An unspoken corollary, understood by all: if this meant war; let it come. "

— Geoffrey Perret, historian, author of *Lincoln's War*

CONFEDERATE AND UNION SOLDIERS

Although the South had fewer soldiers and resources than the North, it had strong military commanders such as Robert E. Lee. One of Lincoln's biggest problems was finding good leaders for the Union army. On both sides, many of the soldiers were young and inexperienced. Some were even in their teens. This chart compares the two groups.

Farmer and soldier Edmund Ruffin is said to have fired the first shot against Fort Sumter

	Confederate Soldiers	Union Soldiers
Who were they?	Farmers, mechanics, students	Farmers, factory workers, recent immigrants, escaped enslaved Africans, and freedmen
Who provided their supplies?	Provided their own supplies	Union army
Uniforms	Gray jackets and soft felt hats with wide brims	Regulation blue wool uniforms and leather-billed caps
Rations	• Fatback (a strip of fat and fatty meat) • Cornbread • Buttermilk or cider	• Salt pork • Hardtack (hard biscuit) • Dried peas • Coffee and sugar
Ammunition	Muskets with no cartridge boxes, ammunition in pockets	Muskets with cartridge boxes slung over their shoulders

The first Union shot at Fort Sumter was fired by Captain Abner Doubleday.

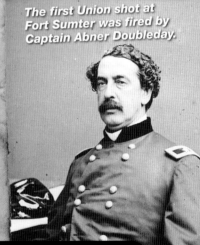

freedmen: *African Americans who had been freed from slavery*

cartridge boxes: *packages containing bullets and gunpowder*

 What does it take to motivate soldiers in a war?

Take Note

The Battle of Fort Sumter blasts into the #7 spot. As the first battle of the Civil War, it marked the end of compromise and discussion between the North and the South. It was the point of no return. War had begun.

• Which do you think is more of a defining moment — the event that marks the start of a war or the event that ends the war? Why?

6 SHERMAN'S MA

An engraving of F.O.C. Darley's General Sherman's March to the Sea Through Georgia, 1864

RCH TO THE SEA

HEADLINE: The South Burns as General Sherman Advances! — November 15 to December 22, 1864

IMPACT: The Confederacy's resources and civilian morale are destroyed.

At the beginning of July 1863, the South suffered two major defeats at the hands of the Union. One was at the Battle of Gettysburg in Union-held territory. The other was at Vicksburg. This was a Confederate fort that protected Southern supply routes along the Mississippi River.

On September 2, 1864, after a long siege, Major General William T. Sherman captured Atlanta, Georgia. Within a week, he ordered the citizens to leave the city. Then he set up camp.

Sherman was under the command of General Ulysses S. Grant (then General in Chief). He was told to go to Alabama, but he marched to Savannah, Georgia, instead. Sherman's army had limited supplies. He studied the census to find out where the centers of population and the farming areas were, so his soldiers could find food along the way.

Sherman persuaded President Lincoln and General Grant that the march to Savannah, a major port near the Atlantic Ocean, was a good idea. On November 15, Sherman left Atlanta in flames, after ordering the destruction of its railways, supply depots, public buildings, and factories. His march to the sea began. His Union forces moved quickly through the South, waging a "total war" on civilians as well as on military targets. Sherman believed this would help bring a quicker end to the war. But the destruction of property, food, and other supplies by Sherman's army caused great damage.

Sherman's march to the sea ended on December 22, when he entered Savannah unopposed.

---

morale: spirits
depots: warehouses; storage spaces

SHERMAN'S MARCH TO THE SEA

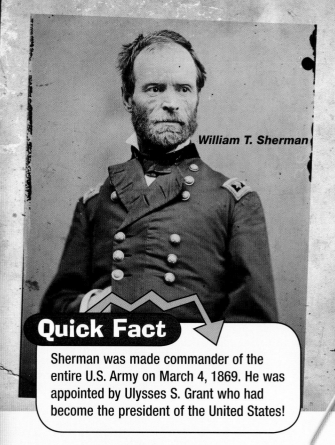

William T. Sherman

MAKING NEWS!

Sherman left Atlanta with 60,000 troops, divided into two wings. They marched to the east — leaving two wide paths of destruction throughout Georgia. They targeted rail lines, bridges, factories, and storage depots. They burned homes, public buildings, plantations, and small farms. Sherman's forces took most of the food that the people had saved up for the winter, burning what they could not eat or carry away. This was Sherman's policy of total war. He wanted to destroy the morale of people in the South.

DEFINING MOMENT

Sherman's army reached the sea on December 10, 1864. They were near Savannah, but Fort McAllister still defended the city. Sherman sent a division to take the fort on December 13. The Confederate forces fought on — they did not want to give up the city. Eventually, they had no choice but to flee, and Sherman entered the city on December 22.

Quick Fact

Sherman was made commander of the entire U.S. Army on March 4, 1869. He was appointed by Ulysses S. Grant who had become the president of the United States!

IN THE END ...

Sherman's march to the sea helped end the war. Some people believed that what Sherman did was right. They felt it was the only way to subdue the South. Others felt that the destruction of the South during the march was much too harsh. Sherman started a new kind of modern warfare — total war. In the South, bitterness against his tactics and against the North would last for decades — even until today for some people. Total war would also become the practice in modern warfare for the next century.

---

subdue: *conquer; gain control over*

 What are some other incidents of total war since Sherman's March to the Sea?

Sherman's troops dismantle artillery after capturing Fort McAllister.

The Expert Says...

"He made a desert of the land through which he passed, destroying major Confederate sources of supply for Southern armies."

— Gary Gallagher, Professor of History, University of Virginia

REMEMBERING SHERMAN

Read this excerpt from the wartime diary of Eliza Andrews, a young girl from Georgia.

About three miles from Sparta we struck the "burnt country," as it is well named by the [local people] and I could well understand the wrath and desperation of these poor people. ... The fields were trampled down and the roads were lined with the carcasses of horses, hogs, and cattle that the invaders, unable to consume or carry off with them, had wantonly shot down, to starve out the people and prevent them from making their crops. The stench in some places was unbearable ...

Crowds of [our] soldiers were tramping over the road in both directions. It was like traveling through the streets of a populous town all day. They were mostly on foot, and I saw numbers on the roadside greedily eating raw turnips, meat skins, parched corn — anything they could find, even picking up the loose grains that Sherman's horses had left.

wrath: *strong anger*
wantonly: *needlessly, often unprovoked*

Atlanta, Georgia, was in ruins after Sherman's army passed through.

They will long remember Sherman
   And his steaming columns free —
They will long remember Sherman
   Marching to the sea.

— American writer Herman Melville

Quick Fact

Sherman sent a telegram to Lincoln two days after taking Savannah. Lincoln's Christmas gift was the city of Savannah and 25,000 bales of cotton!

Take Note

Sherman's march is #6 on our list. It was a defining moment that helped to bring a faster end to the war. It also changed the nature of modern warfare, introducing the practice of total war.
- Do you think that Sherman's tactics of total war were justified? Why or why not?

? How do you think you would have reacted if you were from Georgia and saw the scene that Eliza described?

Soldiers and cannons of the Union's Independent Battery "E" Light Artillery are shown in this photo. Over 50,000 shells were fired at the Battle of Antietam!

TIETAM

HEADLINE: Bloodiest One-Day Battle of the Civil War — September 17, 1862

IMPACT: After the Confederate retreat, President Lincoln decided to free enslaved Africans in the South.

In September 1862, Confederate soldiers, under General Robert E. Lee, invaded Union territory. On the evening of September 16, the armies of the North and the South both prepared for battle.

The next day, the armies fought near Antietam Creek, not far from Sharpsburg, Maryland. It was the first major battle of the Civil War fought on Union soil. The battle began in the fog at dawn. The Confederate forces were west of Antietam Creek; the Union forces east of it. The armies attacked again and again. The fighting ended after 12 hours and the armies buried their dead.

There was no clear-cut victory, but the Confederates withdrew to Virginia. The invasion of the Union territory was stopped. Five days later, Lincoln wrote the draft for the Emancipation Proclamation. He couldn't free enslaved Africans because the Constitution did not grant him the power. But as president, he was commander in chief of the armed forces. He could seize enemy property — and enslaved Africans were considered property! The Emancipation Proclamation became law on January 1, 1863.

MAKING NEWS!

The Battle of Antietam was the bloodiest day of the Civil War. Over 23,000 people were killed or wounded. Eighty-two percent of soldiers in the First Texas Infantry were killed, wounded, or missing. Six generals, three from each side, were killed. Other battles had heavier losses, but they lasted more than one day.

DEFINING MOMENT

The day after Antietam, the Confederates retreated. Their invasion of the Union was halted. General McClellan, who was commander of the Union army at the time, could have followed them. He didn't — and missed his chance of possibly defeating Lee's weakened forces. McClellan was very good at preparing for battle, but he failed to follow through when he had the advantage over the enemy. Two months after Antietam, Lincoln fired McClellan.

IN THE END ...

Antietam was not a clear-cut Union victory, but it changed the Civil War. The battle halted the Southern offensive and General Lee lost hope of support from European countries who didn't want to back a loser. There was more confidence in the North. After the start of the Civil War, President Lincoln had been waiting for a victory before freeing enslaved Africans in the South. When the Confederates withdrew from Antietam, the president decided the moment had come. On January 1, 1863, he issued the Emancipation Proclamation, which freed all enslaved Africans in the South.

President Lincoln (left) meets with General McClellan to discuss battle strategies.

Quick Fact

The site of the Battle of Antietam is now a national park.

The Expert Says...

"[The Emancipation Proclamation] was a symbol and a commitment that changed the nature of the war. From then on, everyone knew that a Northern victory would mean the end of slavery."

— Don E. Fehrenbacher, Stanford University

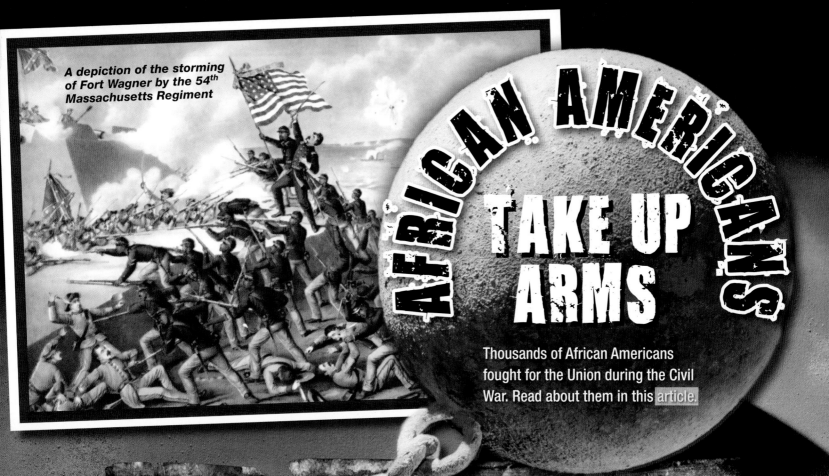

A depiction of the storming of Fort Wagner by the 54th Massachusetts Regiment

AFRICAN AMERICANS TAKE UP ARMS

Thousands of African Americans fought for the Union during the Civil War. Read about them in this article.

Before the Emancipation Proclamation, there were only a few African-American regiments in the Union army. Afterward, there were as many as 180,000 African-American soldiers in uniform.

African Americans served in all-black regiments, usually led by white officers. They earned $10.00 per month but $3.00 was taken off for clothing. White soldiers earned $13.00 per month — with no deductions. Because of this, some African-American regiments chose to serve with no pay. They did not want to accept lower pay than whites. One group that served without pay was the famous 54th Massachusetts Regiment. Its leader was Colonel Robert Gould Shaw, the son of white abolitionists.

In July 1863, the 54th spearheaded an assault on Fort Wagner in South Carolina. The regiment gained worldwide praise for its heroic attack even though it was not a success. Shaw was killed leading the charge. Nearly half of the regiment was wiped out — killed, wounded, or captured.

By the end of the war, more than 32,000 African-American soldiers had given their lives for the Union. The 54th regiment continued to serve. It is still famous today — thanks to the movie *Glory*.

? How would you react knowing that you were being paid little more than half of what someone else was paid for doing the same job?

Take Note

The Battle of Antietam ranks #5. It lasted only one day, but it was the deadliest day of the entire war. Even though the Union did not have a clear victory, the Confederates were forced to retreat. This was a defining moment — it gave Lincoln the chance to issue the Emancipation Proclamation.
• What do you think the headlines would be like in the North and in the South on January 1, 1863?

5   4   3   2   1

This painting by Charles McBarrow shows the 1st Battalion of the U.S. Infantry fighting its way up the steep slope to the top of the Confederate lines at Vicksburg, Mississippi, May 19, 1863.

FIRST AT VICKSBURG—COURTESY OF US ARMY CENTER OF MILITARY HISTORY

CKSBURG

HEADLINE: Vicksburg Falls! North Controls Mississippi River — July 4, 1863

IMPACT: Southern supply lines were cut off.

The Battle of Vicksburg took place in the spring of 1863. It was two years into the American Civil War. Thousands of soldiers, on both sides, had already died.

A main Union target in the South was Vicksburg, Mississippi. The city controlled supply routes along the Mississippi River. First the Union general, Ulysses S. Grant, tried to take Vicksburg from the west. He led 40,000 troops through forests and swamps. They were shot at by Confederate troops and gave up after weeks of trying.

Then General Grant decided to take the city from the east. His troops tried digging a canal to bypass a bend in the river where the Confederates could fire upon them. This didn't work either. The canal kept filling up with water and sand. The Union troops gave up this plan after weeks of being fired upon.

In mid-April 1863, Union ships managed to slip past the Confederate forces at night. On land, Grant's forces planned to take the city from the rear. They eventually surrounded Vicksburg and mounted a major assault on May 22. When that failed, they lay siege to the city. They cut off its supplies, used explosives, and continued to bombard it. The Battle of Vicksburg lasted more than a month and a half.

BATTLE OF VICKSBURG

MAKING NEWS!

The Battle of Vicksburg was part of the larger Vicksburg Campaign. More than half of the Confederate soldiers had died in the fighting that led to the Battle of Vicksburg. Grant asked the Confederate General John C. Pemberton to surrender before the siege, to spare the lives of his men. He would not. The North's attack on Vicksburg lasted for 47 days before the city fell. It is estimated that Grant's forces suffered more than 10,000 casualties to the Confederacy's 9,000.

DEFINING MOMENT

The loss of Vicksburg was a critical defeat for the South. The fort at Vicksburg controlled the Mississippi River. The South had used the river to move supplies and to prevent the North from moving theirs. The North gained control of supply routes in the South. It also divided the South, cutting off Arkansas, Louisiana, and Texas from the rest of the Confederacy.

? Vicksburg is located atop high bluffs beside the Mississippi River. What advantage did this give the defenders of Vicksburg? What disadvantages did the city face?

IN THE END ...

President Lincoln promoted General Grant for taking Vicksburg, and Grant became commander of all the Union forces. The fall of Vicksburg, along with the South's defeat at Gettysburg, was the beginning of the end for the South. The Confederates began to run short of supplies. They could no longer compete with the North.

Quick Fact

The Vicksburg National Cemetery was established in 1866. It contains more than 18,000 graves, of which over 12,000 are unknown. Soldiers from the Civil War, the Spanish-American War, World War I, World War II, and the Korean War are buried here.

The bodies of fallen soldiers are prepared for burial.

The Expert Says...

"The Campaign of Vicksburg was of utmost importance to the cause of the Union. It took a Confederate army from the field ... and freed Grant's army for other operations. It cut the Confederacy in two and opened a highway for trade between the Middle West and the outside world.

— Gary Gallagher, Professor of History, University of Virginia

Born to Lead

John C. Pemberton, commander of the Confederates at Vicksburg, and Ulysses S. Grant, the Union commander, once fought in the same American army during the Mexican-American War. Read the profiles of these two generals.

John C. Pemberton is best known for leading the South at Vicksburg. But he was actually a Northerner, born in Philadelphia! He was deeply loyal to the South because of his Southern-born wife. He joined the Confederate army at the beginning of the Civil War.

Although many in the South were angry at the idea of a Northerner leading their army, Pemberton was promoted in 1862. Jefferson Davis, president of the Confederacy, instructed Pemberton to guard Vicksburg at all costs. He did just that. When his troops ran out of food, they were forced to eat rats and tree bark. Ammunition was limited, but Pemberton continued to fight the North. Many of his men died of disease, hunger, and exhaustion.

Pemberton was a strong leader, but he could not defeat Grant's army. After the war, Pemberton retired from the military. He died in Philadelphia on July 13, 1881.

Ulysses S. Grant: During the Civil War, Grant rose faster and higher through the army than any other officer. He even went on to become the 18th president of the United States.

Grant was eager to fight for the North in the Civil War. In 1862, his troops captured Fort Henry and Fort Donelson — the first major victories for the Union army. Grant also led his soldiers to triumph at the Battle of Shiloh in April 1862. After his success at Vicksburg, he became a hero in the North. In 1865, he accepted the surrender of Robert E. Lee in Appomattox Court House in central Virginia.

Grant was elected president in 1868. While in office, he worked hard to protect the rights of African Americans.

John Clifford Pemberton
(1814-1881)

Ulysses S. Grant
(1822-1885)

Quick Fact

Appomattox Court House was the name of the village where Lee surrendered. In 1892, Appomattox Court House became part of the new town of Appomattox. Today, the place is a national historic park.

Take Note

Vicksburg takes the #4 spot. It was one of the Civil War's most decisive battles. A clear victory for the North, it was a defining moment that changed the course of the war. It led to the destruction of supply lines in the South, and its eventual defeat.
• What did you learn about General Grant from his campaign to take Vicksburg? What three words would you use to describe him?

The 50th Regiment Pennsylvania
Infantry at Gettysburg, Pennsylvania

TTYSBURG

HEADLINE: Hope for a Confederate Victory in the North Crushed!
July 3, 1863

IMPACT: The South retreated — never to invade the North again.

In June 1863, the Confederate army headed to the North for a second time. General Lee hoped that a victory by the South would cause discontent in the North and lead to calls for peace. His army crossed into Pennsylvania late in the month. This was at the same time that Vicksburg, Mississippi, was under siege in the South.

On June 30, a group of Lee's soldiers were heading toward the small town of Gettysburg. They were interested in a supply of shoes they had heard about. Soldiers who had marched long distances and were far from home were likely looking to replace their worn shoes and boots.

Close to town, the Confederates spotted a column of Union cavalry that was also heading to Gettysburg. Both sides called for reinforcements.

The battle began on July 1. For three days, the two armies clashed. The North had the advantage. They had about 90,000 troops to the South's 75,000. The turning point came on July 3 when Lee ordered General Pickett to charge the middle of the Union lines. Pickett's Charge, as this attack became known, was a deadly mistake — one from which the Confederates would not recover.

GETTYSBURG REGIMENT—LOC, LC-DIG-CWPB-03896

35

BATTLE OF GETTYSBURG

MAKING NEWS!

The Battle of Gettysburg began on July 1, 1863. When the Confederate army captured the town, the Union forces retreated to the hills south of Gettysburg. They quickly took up position on Cemetery Ridge. The Confederates held a lower line of hills about half a mile away.

Quick Fact

Cemetery Ridge was well-named — thousands would die there during the battle.

DEFINING MOMENT

The turning point of the battle came on July 3. Under the command of General Pickett, 13,000 soldiers charged across an open field. Union cannon and rifle fire rained down on them. The Confederate forces were torn apart and forced to retreat. The battle was a bloodbath. The North had 23,000 casualties. The South lost even more — 28,000 soldiers lay dead or wounded. That was a third of Lee's forces.

? How do the casualties and outcome of this battle compare with the Battle of Antietam on page 26?

The Expert Says...

"[Pickett's Charge is] the ultimate example of the Civil War soldier's bravery and willingness to sacrifice his life for a cause.

— Earl J. Hess, Civil War historian

IN THE END ...

The Union army failed to finish off the Confederates, but the Confederates retreated to Virginia and did not return to the North again. In November, President Lincoln spoke at the dedication of a cemetery at Gettysburg. It was a powerful speech that called for "a new birth of freedom" and ended with a plea for the fight to continue so that, as Lincoln said, "… government of the People, by the People, for the People, shall not perish from the earth."

Quick Fact

The Gettysburg Address became one of the most famous speeches in American history. It is a tribute to the soldiers who died at Gettysburg. But it is also a tribute to the ideals that the North believed they were fighting for — liberty, equality, and democracy.

Lincoln called on the living to be "dedicated" to the "unfinished work" of those who died at Gettysburg.

In Their Own Words

Following are **eyewitness accounts** of the Battle of Gettysburg, from journal archives

JULY 1

As for myself, I had scarcely reached the front door, when, on looking up the street, I saw some of the men on horseback. I scrambled in, slammed shut the door, and hastening to the sitting room, peeped out between the shutters.

What a horrible sight! There they were — human beings! Clad almost in rags, covered with dust, riding wildly, pell-mell down the hill toward our home! Shouting, yelling ... and firing right and left.

I was fully persuaded that the Rebels had actually come at last. What they would do with us was a fearful question to my young mind.

— Fifteen-year-old Tillie Pierce lived in Gettysburg. She was sent home from school as the Confederate soldiers arrived in the village.

JULY 2

We ran like wild cattle. ... My dead and wounded were then nearly as great in number as those still on duty. They literally covered the ground. ... The blood stood in puddles in some places on the rocks; the ground was soaked in blood.

— Colonel William C. Oates, 15th Alabama, Confederate Army

JULY 3

The next morning was the Fourth of July, but it seemed at the time to those who were at Gettysburg, a somber and terrible anniversary with the indescribable horrors of the field. ... The army did not know the extent of the victory; the nation did not realize as yet what had been done. The armies were still watching each other.

— Lieutenant Jesse Bowman Young, 3rd Army Corps, Union army

hastening: *hurrying*
pell-mell: *in confusion*

Take Note

The Battle of Gettysburg takes the #3 spot. The Union victory was solid proof that the North could defeat the South. It was a significant moment of the war. The Emancipation Proclamation, issued months earlier, began to take effect. As Union soldiers moved into the South, enslaved Africans were freed.
• Read Lincoln's Gettysburg Address honoring those who died during the battle. Compare it with a

Confederate General Robert E. Lee. In the background is the home of Wilmer and Virginia McLean in Appomattox Court House, where Lee surrendered.

GENERAL LEE

HEADLINE: Grant Accepts Lee's Surrender — April 9, 1865

IMPACT: It ended the American Civil War.

By 1863, the Civil War was already drawing to a close. The South had lost two major battles — one at Gettysburg in Pennsylvania; the other at Vicksburg in Mississippi. The Confederate troops could not hold out much longer.

In March 1864, President Lincoln named Ulysses S. Grant commander of all the Union forces. Grant had not only been successful at Vicksburg but in late November, 1863, had defeated Southern forces at Chattanooga, Tennessee. Next Grant went against Confederate General Robert E. Lee in Virginia. At the same time, General Sherman was leading his Union troops to the sea, using the tactics of total war and leaving a trail of destruction throughout the South.

In June 1864, Grant's army arrived at Petersburg, just south of Richmond, Virginia. The Union army could not break through the Confederate defenses. They dug trenches and settled in for a long siege. There was a 10-month standoff. In the end, it was Lee's Confederates who could not hold out. They tried to move to the west, but Union troops cut them off. In early April 1865, General Lee knew it was hopeless. "Then there is nothing left me but to go and see General Grant," said Lee, "and I would rather die a thousand deaths."

? In the last part of this quotation, Lee is rewording a famous line from Shakespeare. What do you think he means by this?

SURRENDER OF GENERAL LEE

MAKING NEWS!

Just before noon on April 9, 1865, General Lee sent a white flag with a note to General Grant. The two generals met that afternoon in Appomattox Court House to arrange the surrender. Lee requested that his soldiers be allowed to keep their horses as they would need them for plowing. Grant agreed and also provided rations for the hungry soldiers. The two generals shook hands and Lee rode off to say goodbye to his troops.

Quick Fact

Lee's white flag was actually a white towel because he couldn't find a flag.

DEFINING MOMENT

Lee was commander in chief of all the Confederate forces. In theory, he could have surrendered on behalf of all the Southern armies. But he only surrendered as commander of the Army of North Virginia. Even so, this was a very significant moment of the Civil War. Lee's surrender was a signal to the Confederate armies that the war was lost. However, news of Lee's surrender did not reach some of the other Confederate troops until much later. Troop surrenders continued until May 26, 1865.

 Why do you think it took so long for news to reach the troops?

IN THE END ...

This was the most costly war in American history. Over 600,000 people died, and the Southern states were left in ruins. However, the war put an end to slavery. The 13th Amendment of the Constitution, ratified on December 6, 1865, banned slavery in the United States. But racial discrimination continued. Another 100 years passed before African Americans gained equal rights under the law, with the passing of the Civil Rights Act in 1964.

ratified: *made official*

Slavery ended but racial discrimination continued. Why do you think this was?

The Surrender of General Lee to General Grant, *April 9, 1865, a painting by Louis Guillaume*

The Expert Says...

" In the long run, Northern superiority in supplies and men was decisive. That Southern armies remained in the field and took a toll from their opponents until the spring of 1865 is a remarkable achievement. ... "

— Gary Gallagher, Professor of History, University of Virginia

FALL OF THE CONFEDERACY
BY THE NUMBERS

Check out this fact chart for more information about the surrender of the South.

$3.3 BILLION
Total cost of the war for both governments, in 1860 dollars

$1.5 BILLION
Estimated cost of destruction in the South, in 1860 dollars

1,000,000
The number of Union troops at the end of the Civil War

110,000
The number of Union troops Grant had at Appomattox Court House

100,000 (OR FEWER)
The number of Confederate troops present for duty at the end of the Civil War

26,000
The approximate number of Confederate soldiers who surrendered between April 9 and April 12.

6
The number of days Lincoln lived after the surrender

3
The number of years before General Ulysses S. Grant is elected president of the United States

Quick Fact
After the surrender, General Sheridan paid Wilmer McLean $20 for the table where General Grant sat when he accepted General Lee's surrender!

Take Note
The surrender of General Lee ranks #2 on our list of most defining Civil War moments. Lee's surrender marked the end of the bloodiest war on American soil.
- Research more about general Robert E. Lee. How important was his role in the Civil War?

1 ELECTION OF

As an outspoken opponent of the expansion of slavery, Lincoln won the Republican Party nomination in May 1860. He was elected president later that year.

ABRAHAM LINCOLN

HEADLINE: Lincoln Becomes 16th President — November 6, 1860

IMPACT: By the time Lincoln was sworn in as president in March 1861, seven states had left the Union.

The election of 1860 was certainly unusual. In some ways, it was two elections — one in the North and another in the South. The antislavery Republican Party ran only one candidate — Abraham Lincoln. Because there was a split in the party over slavery, the Democratic Party ran separate candidates in the North and in the South. There was also the new Constitutional Union Party, which ran its own candidate.

Abraham Lincoln was the clear winner in the election. He had slightly less than 40 percent of the popular vote. But he took all but two states in the North plus Oregon and California. The Democratic candidate in the South took every state except for three border states. These were won by the Constitutional Union Party.

The election of Abraham Lincoln was the most defining moment of the Civil War era. Within months, the nation was at war. During the election campaign, Lincoln promised he would do nothing to abolish slavery. But Southerners didn't believe him. In December, South Carolina was the first Southern state to withdraw from the Union. More states soon followed to join the Confederacy. To hold the nation together, Lincoln had no choice but to declare war on the Confederates. America was at war with itself!

ELECTION OF ABRAHAM LINCOLN

On February 18, 1861, Jefferson Davis was sworn in as president of the Confederate States on the steps of the Alabama State Capital.

MAKING NEWS!

In the North, people celebrated Lincoln's election. They believed that "Honest Abe" deserved to be in the White House. But the new president had won without getting any votes in the South. Not surprising ... since he wasn't on the ballot. Leaders in the South said that they would never accept Lincoln as president because of his opposition to slavery.

DEFINING MOMENT

Lincoln's election triggered the American Civil War. Within two months of the election, six more states had joined South Carolina and left the Union. Four more states would leave later. In February, Jefferson Davis, a plantation owner and U.S. senator from Mississippi, was sworn in as President of the Confederate States of America. On April 12, the first battle of the Civil War was fought at Fort Sumter.

Quick Fact
In the 1860 election, 81.2 percent of all eligible voters cast a ballot. Women and enslaved Africans were not allowed to vote.

IN THE END ...

The Civil War was a war against fellow Americans, and it was the bloodiest war in U.S. history. The war took a terrible mental toll on Lincoln, but his firm belief in the strength of the American Union was vindicated with a victory for the Union. He is remembered today as one of America's greatest presidents. Abraham Lincoln and George Washington are the two presidents honored on Presidents Day.

vindicated: *defended successfully*

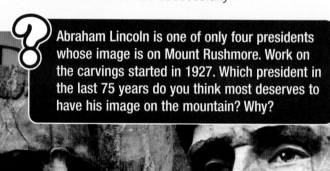

? Abraham Lincoln is one of only four presidents whose image is on Mount Rushmore. Work on the carvings started in 1927. Which president in the last 75 years do you think most deserves to have his image on the mountain? Why?

The Expert Says...

" Republicans celebrated Lincoln's victory in Northern cities — and across the South he was burned in _____ in front of [county] courthouses. "

— Geoffrey C. Ward, *The Civil War: An Illustrated History*

WE ARE NOT ENEMIES

On March 4, 1861, Abraham Lincoln was sworn in as president of the United States. In his inaugural address, he tried to build on his support in the North and soothe fears in the South. Note the appeal to his fellow citizens and the promises that Lincoln made in his speech.

… I have no purpose, directly or indirectly, to interfere with the institution of slavery in the states where it exists. I believe I have no lawful right to do so, and I have no inclination to do so. …

In your hands, my dissatisfied fellow countrymen, and not in mine, is the momentous issue of civil war. The government will not assail you. You have no conflict without yourselves being the aggressors. You have no oath in Heaven to destroy the government, while I shall have the most solemn one to "preserve, protect and defend" it. I am loath to close. We are not enemies, but friends. We must not be enemies. Though passion may have strained, it must not break our bonds of affection. The mystic chords of memory, stretching from every battlefield, and patriot grave, to every living heart and hearthstone, all over this broad land, will yet swell the chorus of the Union, … .

---

assail: *attack*
loath: *reluctant*

 What do you think are some of the shared memories that Lincoln is referring to at the end of his speech?

Quick Fact

Lincoln's speech was sent across the country by telegraph and even pony express. It was then printed in newspapers.

Take Note

The election of Abraham Lincoln takes the #1 position. It led, almost immediately, to the secession of the Southern states. Other earlier events helped build tension between the North and the South but did not lead directly to war as the election did.

• Do you agree that Lincoln's election was the most defining moment of the American Civil War? What arguments would you make for or against this ranking?

We Thought ...

Here are some of the criteria we used in ranking the most defining moments of the Civil War era.

The defining moment:
- Divided the country
- Triggered the start of the war
- Changed the course of the war
- Changed the way war was fought
- Led to a large number of casualties
- Changed American society
- Brought about the end of the war

What Do You Think?

1. Do you agree with our ranking? If you don't, try ranking these defining moments yourself. Justify your ranking with data from your own research and reasoning. You may refer to our criteria, or you may want to draw up your own list of criteria.

2. Here are thee other defining moments we considered but in the end did not include in our top 10 list: Dred Scott Decision, the Second Battle of Bull Run, and the Battle of Chickamauga.
   - Find out more about these moments. Do you think they should have made our list? Give reasons for your response.
   - Are there other defining moments that you think should have made our list? Explain your choices.

Index